Acknowledgements:

My daughters, for being so cool and keeping me young. My son, for being so pure and funny. I love each of you more than words can ever describe.

Every participant in the, *Paris Loves Books* community.♥

Finally, my illustrator, Taiye. He took my vision and made it a reality for me.

www.parislovesbooks.com

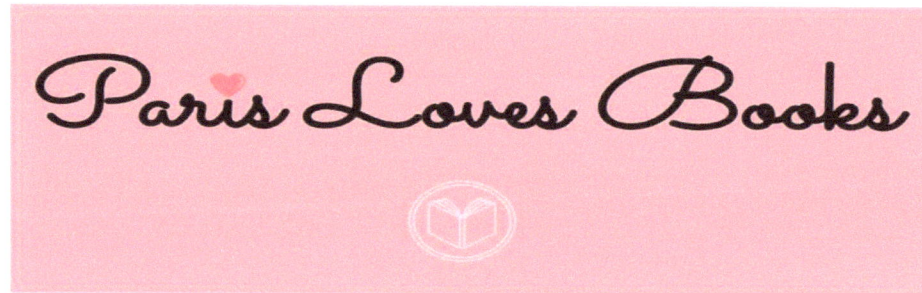

Published by, Paris Loves Books

Chicago, Illinois

Dedicated to my dear late uncle,
Paul "Goodness" Rodgers

My name is Floyd.
I'm 4 years old,
I love to jump and play!

1

My favorite letter
Is the letter F,
Because my name
starts that way.

So many cool words
start with F like

FINGERS,

FUN,

and FOOD.

3

Today I learned a new F word,
That put my mommy in a bad mood!

I heard it on TV, so I thought
it was okay to say.

I couldn't wait to say it
at some point during the day.

Mom was cooking, dad was reading,
and my sisters were having fun.

When the house was finally quiet enough I asked,
"Where the F*CK is everyone?"

7

My mom said, "What?",
my dad said, "Huh?",
and my sisters said, "No way!"

My dad said, "Son",
my mom said, "Boy!"
and my sisters ran away.

10

I was confused, what did I do,
and why was mommy mad?

My mom turned off the stove, grabbed my hand, and said "Son, that word is bad."

"People use these words
to be hurtful or express
the anger they feel.

Sticks and stones can
break your bones, but
hurting people with
words is real."

13

I covered my mouth with both of my hands, because I felt bad about what I said.

14

I apologized to everyone in the house before I went to bed.

The next day I asked, "Are there more bad words that people shouldn't say?" My dad said, "Yes, but you don't need to learn them because we don't speak that way."

16

"Only speak kind words to people, Floyd", my mom said while closing the door.

17

About the author

Chicago resident, Paris Chanel can usually be found doing one of two things: writing or reading. She has been a lover of books for her entire life. Her first book love was, *The Hatchet* by American writer, Gary Paulsen. She finished The Hatchet in two days and realized books are an escape or a way to travel without leaving her room.

She first started writing stories at nine years old. Her childhood dream was to be a published author one day. She would sign her name in the back of books, pretending it was her book signing. Paris did not become serious about being a published author until she became a secretary in a hospital and shared a new story with the nursing crew everyday. They encouraged her to pursue writing professionally. She finally published her first book, *The F Word*, in 2021.

Paris spent years searching for a community of likeminded-creative individuals to engage with. When she couldn't find one, she made her own. *Paris Loves Books* (PLB) was established in 2016 and is an ever-growing community that is one of Paris' pride and joys.

Paris Loves Books

Paris Loves Books is a creative community for book lovers, writers, book reviewers, bloggers, and creatives. The PLB community is a place for creatives to network, share, promote, and acts as an indie author resource. Join the PLB community!

www.parislovesbooks.com
&
@Paris.Loves.Books on all platforms

The End

So from now on, I'll stick to F words more like
FRENCH FRY,
FRAME,
and
FLOOR!

18

www.ingramcontent.com/pod-product-compliance
Lightning Source LLC
Chambersburg PA
CBHW040804300326

41914CB00064B/1604